YELLOW FEVER

by R.A. Shiomi

D1715414

PLAYWRIGHTS CANADA
Toronto

YELLOW FEVER

PLAYWRIGHTS CANADA is the imprint of PLAYWRIGHTS UNION OF CANADA.

PLAYWRIGHTS UNION OF CANADA
8 York Street, 6th Floor
Toronto, Ontario
Canada M5J 1R2
Phone (416) 947-0201

PLAYWRIGHTS UNION OF CANADA operates with generous assistance from the Canada Council, the Ontario Ministry of Citizenship and Culture, the Ontario Arts Council, Alberta Culture, Wintario, Metropolitan Toronto, and the City of Toronto through the Toronto Arts Council.

Front cover photo: Harvey Chao in the Canasian Artists Group/Toronto Free Theatre production of YELLOW FEVER. Cover photo by John To. Cover design by Lisa Dimson. Editor: Ann Jansen

ISBN 0-88754-377-4

First Edition: December 1984

Printed and bound in Canada

YELLOW FEVER was first presented at the Asian American Theater Company, San Francisco, in March, 1982, with the following cast:

SAM Shikaze . . . . A.M. Lai

NANCY Wing . . . . June Mesina

CHUCK Chan . . . . Dennis Dun

Captain KADOTA . . . . John Nishio

Sergeant MACKENZIE . . . . . Bob Martin

Superintendent JAMESON
  and GOLDBERG . . . . . . Blaine Palmer

Directed by Lane Kiyomi Nishikawa

Settings by Lane Kiyomi Nishikawa
and R.A. Shiomi

Lighting by Wilbur Obata

Costumes by Linda Obata

Technical Direction by James B. Chew

Produced by Rick Lee and Tim Wing Wo

Note

The story for YELLOW FEVER was co-conceived by R.A. Shiomi and Marc Hayashi.

YELLOW FEVER was presented in New York in December, 1982, by the Pan Asian Repertory Theater, with the following cast:

SAM Shikaze . . . . Donald Li

NANCY Wing . . . . Freda Foh Shen

CHUCK Chan . . . . Henry Yuk

Captain KADOTA . . . . . . Ernest Abuba

Sergeant MACKENZIE . . . Jeffrey Spolan

ROSIE . . . . Carol Honda

Superintendent JAMESON
  and GOLDBERG . . . . . . James Jenner

Directed by Raul Aranas

Settings by Chris Stapelton

Lighting by Dawn Chiang

Costumes by Lillian Pan

Stage Manager, Eddas M. Bennett

Artistic Director, Tisa Chang

Produced by Tisa Chang

YELLOW FEVER was subsequently presented in
Toronto at Toronto Free Theatre by Canasian
Artists Group in September, 1983, with the
following cast:

SAM Shikaze . . . . Harvey Chao

NANCY Wing . . . . Susan Jay

CHUCK Chan . . . . Mary Lee

Captain KADOTA . . . . Bob Lem

Sergeant MACKENZIE . . . . . Jim Knapp

ROSIE . . . . Brenda Kamino

Superintendent JAMESON

  and GOLDBERG . . . . . Tom MacDonald

Directed by Raul Aranas

Settings by Maya Duncan

Lighting by Dawn Chiang

Costumes by Paul Cheung and Allen Shugar

Produced by Susan Carter, Phillip Ing
and Terry Watada

The Characters:

SAM Shikaze: 45, nisei detective, the hard-boiled loner.

NANCY Wing: 25, attractive and assertive but inexperienced reporter for major Vancouver newspaper.

CHUCK Chan: 32, hip, fast-talking lawyer.

Captain KADOTA: 45, nisei policeman, a man who has lived by the rules and regulations.

Sergeant MACKENZIE: Mid-thirties, a bluff racist.

ROSIE: Late forties, a kibei cafe owner.

Superintendent JAMESON: Mid-fifties, a suave demagogue.

GOLDBERG: Young Japanophile professor.

The Setting:

Powell Street in Vancouver, British Columbia, Canada.

Stage right is an alley way. Centre stage is a raised platform serving as SAM's office. There is an upstage window facing onto the alley way. SAM's chair and desk are on stage right of the platform. There are windows with scrims as the backdrop for the office, with a door in the middle. There is a client's chair, a coat rack, a radio, a filing cabinet and a mirror in the office. Stage left is Rosie's Cafe. There is the cafe entrance upstage left with a kitchen exit curtain stage left of the door. There is a counter along stage left wall with three stools, and a table with two chairs downstage left. There is a coat rack and extra chair extreme

downstage left. In Act Two, the cafe space is
changed to an English-style pub with all the cafe
items removed.

The Time:

Act One: The morning of March 9, 1973.
Act Two: Evening, a few days later.

Performance Style:

Although YELLOW FEVER is definitely a parody of
the detective genre, it should be played with
dramatic realism by the actors/characters in
order to get both the greatest comedic impact and
the dramatic power underlying the comedy.

Note on Generations:

Issei: First generation Japanese Canadian.
Nisei: Second generation Japanese Canadian.
Sansei: Third generation Japanese Canadian.
Kibei: Born in Canada, but lived in Japan for
many years before returning to Canada.

YELLOW FEVER

Act One

SAM appears in a spotlight.

SAM: Monday, March 9th, 1973, I walked
       down to my office on Powell Street.
       It used to be our main strip. Used
       to be snack bars, general stores,
       boarding houses, gambling joints, we
       had it all... That was back in
       forty-one, when I was a kid running
       groceries for Mrs. Sato. World War
       Two came and the government moved us
       out, sent us packing into the
       mountains, herded onto trains and
       dumped off in godforsaken ghost
       towns... After the war it was never
       the same. They didn't let us back
       to the coast till forty-nine, and by
       then we were scattered east of the
       Rockies. A few of us returned, not
       just to Vancouver, but to Powell
       Street... Times have changed, now
       my nisei friends tell me I should
       move downtown, forget the past and
       get a decent job. I just tell them
       I like the local colour... Being a
       private eye doesn't give you that
       nine-to-five respectability, but you
       call your own shots and you don't

have to smile for a living...and that's the way I like it.

> (SAM exits through alley way. Lights come up on the cafe setting. ROSIE is cleaning the counter and humming to herself. GOLDBERG is sitting at the counter. SAM enters through the cafe door)

Hi, Rosie.

ROSIE: Irasshaimas-e. (Welcome.)

SAM: *(to audience as he hangs up his hat and coat)* I stopped in at Rosie's Cafe, for some of her ochazuke (rice soup). My folks died years ago and my sister moved to Toronto, so Rosie's like family to me. *(walks to table, sits)* She's my mama-san, my piece of the rock.

> (ROSIE enters again with tea and ochazuke on tray)

Well Rosie, another Cherry Blossom Bazaar's come and gone eh.

ROSIE: Hai (Yes), one more year goodbye.

SAM: Good weather for a change, huh?

ROSIE: Honto, i tenki desu neh. (Really beautiful weather.) But I no see you at the Bazaar. *(serves food)*

SAM: Domo (Thanks)... I was out of town.

ROSIE: Too bad, you miss everybody.

SAM: Tough luck eh. *(begins eating)*

ROSIE: Hah, I think you hiding. Everyone
            ask, "Shikaze-san doko desuka?
            Shikaze-san nani o shiteruno?"
            ("Where is Shikaze? What's he
            doing?")

SAM: They come down to Powell Street once
            a year and want to know what I been
            up to, eh?

ROSIE: Honto (Really), everybody wants to
            know.

GOLDBERG: *(getting up to leave)* Gochisosamma
            deshita. (Thanks for the soup.)

ROSIE: *(turning to GOLDBERG)* Hai, domo
            arigato gozaimasu. (Yes, thank you
            very much.)

                    *(GOLDBERG goes to coat rack and
                    stands there momentarily before
                    exiting. ROSIE clears the
                    counter)*

            Anatano okasan (Your wife), I saw
            her at the Bazaar. She's still very
            pretty in kimono, neh.

SAM: Not anymore. *(finishes meal and sips
            tea)*

ROSIE: Hontoni, kawaii desho. (Really, very
            pretty.) *(returns to sit at table)*

SAM: Not my wife anymore, remember.

ROSIE: Ah Samu, why don't you try again? Everybody says she is so, how you say, delicato. Her family is high class and she knows ikebana so well neh.

SAM: She always was arranging things.

ROSIE: I remember how excited you were, long time ago.

SAM: A long time ago.

ROSIE: So young and crazy in love.

SAM: It was crazy.

ROSIE: Nani o shimashitaka? (What happened?)

SAM: It was like a fire. We burned out.

ROSIE: What happened? A house burns down, you can build another. Everybody has problems these days. No need to get divorce, like hakujin (white) people.

SAM: We threw in the towel ages ago.

ROSIE: It's hard to find a good wife.

SAM: It's a rough life Rosie.

ROSIE: So neh, but you are not getting younger.

SAM: *(gets up)* You got me there. Old Man Time is the one guy I can't shake... Gochisosama. (Thanks.)

ROSIE: *(walks to coat rack to get his hat and coat)* You are so sad to get old by yourself, no family to take care of you. Look at all the ojisans (old men) living in hotels here; so poor and lonely and stubborn. You gonna be just like them.

SAM: *(takes hat and coat)* That's life Rosie. It ain't so bad, lots of guys grow old, and I always got you.

ROSIE: That's what you always say neh. *(clears table, taking tablecloth)*

SAM: Yeah Rosie, see you later.

> *(SAM exits out cafe door. ROSIE laughs as she clears his table. Lights cross fade to SAM's office. He enters office door)*

Rosie was a real sweetie. She could dish out the advice without expecting me to take it. That was our understanding. *(walks to coat stand to hang up coat and hat)* My ex-wife was still pretty, but she needed the kind of attention I couldn't give her. She had big plans for us, too big for me. *(opens file cabinet to get bottle of Canadian Club)* We split up in sixty-three. Ten years married and ten years apart. *(pours shot and takes sip)* It's been a lot quieter since sixty-three. *(turns on a radio that sits on file cabinet)* Her old man had the dough to keep her going in style. And me?... I had the business.

6

(He takes out folder from
cabinet, sits down at desk,
and lights up cigarette as soft
big band music from the forties
plays on radio. Knock on the
office door, stage left. CHUCK
Chan enters)

CHUCK: You're back.

SAM: Yeah.

CHUCK: What was out in the Fraser Valley?
            (takes off overcoat)

SAM: Con man selling phoney insurance to
            some farming buddies, for their
            strawberries.

CHUCK: Sounds like easy pickings.

SAM: The farmers, or the berries?

CHUCK: (walks to radio) Who cares huh.

SAM: Not you eh.

CHUCK: (switching channels to a pop music
            station) All a matter of priorities,
            Sam. All a matter of priorities.

SAM: So what's up?

CHUCK: (sits down in client's chair) Just
            making my rounds.

SAM: Take advantage of the sunshine and
            fresh air eh.

CHUCK: It's spring, Sam. Ever get the urge to clean this place up? *(turns radio off)* You could even splurge on a new hat. Might do wonders for your image. *(takes SAM's hat off rack and tosses it at him)*

SAM: *(catches hat)* Take it easy, I just got it cleaned.

CHUCK: Some people never change huh.

SAM: What for? *(finds note inside hat)* Hmmm, Beware the Edes of March?

CHUCK: Ides, Sam.

SAM: Huh?

CHUCK: Ides of March, it's from *Julius Caesar*...you know, Shakespeare.

SAM: So what?

CHUCK: It's the warning an old man gave to Caesar.

SAM: Go on, it's just getting interesting.

CHUCK: The Republicans knocked him off on the Ides, that's the fifteenth.

SAM: Yah ought'a be a detective, Chuck.

CHUCK: Not worth my time, least not the way you do it.

SAM: Yeah, you wouldn't spend a week saving a few bucks for a bunch of nisei farmers, would yah Chuck?

CHUCK: You're too good for your own good.
           How much you charge those buddies?
           A hundred plus expenses? For a week's
           work? You run your business like a
           community service.

SAM: That's my business.

CHUCK: Having roots is fine, but you gotta
           grow too. With your talent and my
           savvy, we could make a killing.

SAM: (studying note) Tell me about it.

CHUCK: You're the detective, I'm the lawyer.
           You bring 'em in, I get 'em out. We
           get them coming and going. Like this
           divorce case I got now. Woman's
           suing her millionaire hubby for half
           the bundle. All we have to do is get
           some of his affairs in black and
           white.

SAM: Sure, but right now I'd rather figure
           out this little note.

CHUCK: So who's been fiddling with your hat?

SAM: Couple of people...naahhh.

CHUCK: What naahh?

SAM: Nothin'.

CHUCK: Somebody drops a threat on you and
           it's nothing?

SAM: Not yet.

CHUCK: Let me drop something else on you, care of my rounds. The Cherry Blossom Queen has disappeared.

SAM: Disappeared?

CHUCK: Gotta keep in touch Sam.

SAM: So who's been spreading the gossip this time?

CHUCK: Sergeant Mackenzie. He says she didn't make it home from the Bazaar Saturday night. Her father's been calling the station by the hour. Funny thing is, Mackenzie and a couple of other cops dropped by the Church that night, so she disappeared right out from under their noses.

SAM: They got big noses.

CHUCK: And they've put Kadota on the case.

SAM: Great, they're sending their tokens in after us eh.

CHUCK: This is still the ghetto to them.

SAM: Funny, Rosie didn't say anything.

CHUCK: Kudo's trying to keep it quiet right now.

SAM: Gordon Kudo's kid is the Queen?

CHUCK: Yeah, cute kid.

SAM: Too cute... You check her friends out?

CHUCK: I'm not even on the case yet. This is your turf, I take over in court. Anyway I got business to take care of.

SAM: Make hay while the sun shines eh.

CHUCK: *(heading for door)* That's only for farmers, Sam.

SAM: Yeah, thanks for the tip. *(turns radio to soft music)*

CHUCK: Anytime.

SAM: Hey, how about dinner at Rosie's?

CHUCK: Sure, see you later.

(CHUCK exits out office door. SAM stands by the cabinet, talking to audience)

SAM: I had to give Chuck credit. He ran a classy operation downtown and still had time for the people over here. *(gets up to get another file folder out of cabinet)* The dope on the Kudo kid was that she was some disco queen turning hakujin, hoping her crown would launch her into the mainstream modeling scene. *(sits down at desk)* I checked through her family file 'cause I had a hunch her old man would be calling me soon enough.

(Phone rings. SAM turns off radio before picking up the phone)

Sam Shikaze here... Hi Gordon... I
just heard... It's my business to
know, Gordon.

> *(Knock on the office door.
> NANCY Wing enters)*

NANCY: Hi, I'm Nancy Wing of the *Sun*.

SAM: *(looks up)* Sorry, I'm busy.

NANCY: I thought you were Shikaze.

SAM: Huh?... *(into phone)* Gomen, Gordon
(Excuse me, Gordon), of course I'll
take the case... So when did you
last see her?

NANCY: *(walking around office)* Oh, about
six o'clock.

SAM: *(into phone)* You didn't think of
taking her home?

NANCY: Her boyfriend usually did that.

SAM: What's his name?

NANCY: John Richardson.

SAM: He belonged to the Phi Geta Bamma
frat eh.

NANCY: That's Beta Gamma, *(standing by
window)* and uh, don't you find it
stuffy in here?

SAM: *(to NANCY)* Doesn't open... *(into
phone)* My window, Gordon... Forget
it.

NANCY: No problem. *(bangs on frame)*

SAM: *(to NANCY)* Hey, take it easy!

NANCY: It's just stuck.

SAM: *(into phone)* Gomen, Gordon, I know you got a right to be upset.

NANCY: *(gets window open a little)* See, it'll open some.

SAM: That's the way it is these days.

NANCY: It's better that way, isn't it?

SAM: *(into phone but looking at NANCY)* Who knows, I'll get started on the case, and I'll get the window fixed. *(hangs up phone)*

NANCY: So you're the Sam Shikaze. *(extends hand)*

SAM: That's the name on the door kid. *(ignores her hand)*

NANCY: Quaint place you have here.

SAM: Most people call it crummy. *(closes window)* What can I do for yah?

NANCY: You could let in some fresh air.

SAM: You're fresh enough for me kid. *(lets down venetian blind)*

NANCY: Are you always so friendly?

SAM: Not to strangers.

(NANCY walks back to desk and sits opposite SAM)

So what brings a big-time reporter down here?

NANCY: What do you mean by that?

SAM: Your kind only drop by when we turn out in kimonos.

NANCY: Anything else worth covering?

SAM: Guess not eh, just the skid row winos and us quiet Japanese.

NANCY: Not even many of you left, are there?

SAM: Let's get to the point.

NANCY: *(pause)* What's happened to Miss Cherry Blossom?

SAM: The grapevine's turned into a wire service eh.

NANCY: We have our contacts.

SAM: So what's Miss Cherry Blossom got to do with me?

NANCY: The inside story. They say you know when a twig breaks on Powell Street.

SAM: You're barking up the wrong tree kid... You ought'a call the Gardeners' Association.

NANCY: I can see you're going to be a great help.

SAM: Help yourself, if you can open that
             window I'm sure you can kick in a
             few more doors.

NANCY: *(stands up)* I will if I have to.

SAM: Good luck.

NANCY: *(pause)* You wouldn't have a clue, or
             a suspect, would you? Somebody with
             an axe to grind?

SAM: *(looking up)* Listen kid, I'm getting
             an axe to grind.

NANCY: I mean, could she be the victim of
             feuding in the ghetto?

SAM: Where?

NANCY: The...ghetto... I mean Powell Street.

SAM: You know, for a second there you
             sounded like a princess in a garbage
             dump.

NANCY: Sorry, I didn't mean anything.

SAM: Sure, no water off your back eh.
             Course it's not all still waters
             running deep down here. Nobody says
             so, but there are some women who'd
             like to see Miss Cherry Blossom take
             a flying leap.

NANCY: Don't humour me, I came for the facts.

SAM: I thought they spoke for themselves.

NANCY: *(walks to door)* Hell of a lot more
                useful than some people.

SAM: Yeah, then why don't you just run
                down the facts.

NANCY: Watch out, I might run you over.

SAM: I'll keep that in mind.

                *(NANCY opens door only to have
                Sergeant MACKENZIE and Captain
                KADOTA enter)*

MACKENZIE: Hello Sammy, got hired help now?
                Yuh must be movin' up in the world.

NANCY: Watch it, buddy, I'm from the *Sun*.

SAM: Look out, Sarge, she might kick your
                drawers open.

KADOTA: Sam, we just dropped by to tell you
                we can handle this one.

SAM: What one, Kenji?

KADOTA: Captain, Sam...remember? I didn't
                get kicked out of cadet school. I
                made it.

SAM: That was a while back, Kenbo. What
                yah been doing lately?

KADOTA: More than cleaning out dirty laundry.

SAM: Least the boys come clean when I'm
                done.

MACKENZIE: Don't let him play about, Captain.

KADOTA: Listen Sam, stay out of the Kudo case, wakaru (understand)?

MACKENZIE: What's that, Captain?

KADOTA: Nothing, Mackenzie.

SAM: Don't worry Sarge, we're just playin' Japanese.

NANCY: He's a real character, isn't he?

(KADOTA turns to NANCY)

SAM: By the way, Kenji, this is my Girl Sunday.

NANCY: I'm Nancy Wing, a reporter for the *Sun*.

KADOTA: You better look somewhere else for your story. *(sits in client's chair)*

NANCY: Wait a minute.

KADOTA: This is off the record, understand.

NANCY: We're obviously not speaking the same language.

KADOTA: You Chinese?

NANCY: *(pulling out microphone)* Does that bother you?

KADOTA: Shut that off! *(turns to SAM)* Get rid of her, Sam.

SAM: Come on, Kenji, I was just getting used to her.

KADOTA: Okay, Miss Reporter, we've nothing to hide. Just keep out of the way of our investigation.

NANCY: So who's in the way?

KADOTA: Sam, listen to me, we deal with the criminals, you stick to the peep holes and petty thefts. None of this, "We can take care of our own".

SAM: Should've told Sarge. He might have sneezed and blown the case wide open.

MACKENZIE: Now that's a bit much, Sammy!

KADOTA: For the good of the community.

SAM: We got a reputation to live down, eh?

KADOTA: We're Nihonjin nah. (We're Japanese, right.)

MACKENZIE: We're what, Captain?

SAM: First time I ever heard you say "we" about us, Kenji.

KADOTA: Well I'm telling you now.

MACKENZIE: Aye, we're givin' yah fair warnin', Sammy.

SAM: Real considerate of you boys.

KADOTA: This is no time for wisecracks!

SAM: Somebody leaning on you?

KADOTA: Nobody pushes me--

SAM: Sounds like election year to me.
                Mayor's out to clean out the ghettos,
                right kid?...with Captain Kadota
                leading the parade.

MACKENZIE: About time eh.

KADOTA: Mackenzie!

MACKENZIE: I was just--

KADOTA: Interrupting me!

SAM: You two want to step outside?

KADOTA: Sam, I'm telling you, keep your nose
                out of this one.

SAM: Sorry Kenji, Kudo's already hired me.

KADOTA: Bakka! (You're crazy!)

MACKENZIE: Huh, Captain?

KADOTA: Nothing.

MACKENZIE: *(to himself)* Lot of bloomin' noise
                for nothin'.

SAM: We're just shootin' the breeze,
                Sarge.

MACKENZIE: Aye, well yuh better watch yer step
                Sammy, yer Chinese cousins may be
                behind this one here.

SAM: Sounds like you're hot on the trail.

KADOTA: We're doing our job.

MACKENZIE: Aye, we are at that. Ever heard of the Hong Kong Tong Connection?

SAM: That connected to the French one?

NANCY: Some detective we have here.

KADOTA: We've reliable sources that say the Tongs are expanding their operations, muscling in on your territory.

SAM: Didn't know we had anything left to take down here.

MACKENZIE: We all know how the Chinese like to trade in women.

NANCY: Now wait a second, buddy. Another line like that and you'll be on the front page and out of a job.

KADOTA: Watch your mouth, Mackenzie.

SAM: You talked to Chuck yet?

MACKENZIE: We have out doubts about him too, 'cause he's one of 'em, ain't he?

SAM: One of who?

MACKENZIE: Don't muck us about, laddie!

SAM: There yah go, front page splash, "Terror of the Hongs".

MACKENZIE: Tongs, Sammy. Yuh think we're bloomin' idiots, don't cha? Think we ain't capable of doin' our duty here, eh?

SAM: I wasn't at the Bazaar, so I don't know how you blew it.

MACKENZIE: Don't get perky now, we know how to
             deal with your kind.

SAM: So shit or get off the can.

MACKENZIE: *(reaches for SAM)* Why yuh!

KADOTA: *(grabbing MACKENZIE)* That's enough,
             Mackenzie!

SAM: Maybe yah better get a leash, Kenji.

MACKENZIE: *(lunges at SAM again)* By Jesus I'll
             bash his--

KADOTA: *(pulling MACKENZIE back)* Not here!
             (to SAM) And you shut up!

SAM: Sure, if you're finished with the
             small talk.

KADOTA: We are for now, but we'll be around.
             So don't try and get cute, nah.

SAM: I'm too old for that, and I never was
             good lookin'.

                   *(KADOTA and MACKENZIE exit out
                    office door. SAM sits down to
                    continue work at desk. NANCY
                    walks to the door)*

NANCY: You don't let up, do you?

SAM: Can't afford to.

NANCY: Tough guy all the way, eh.

SAM: Any last words, kid?

NANCY: The name's Nancy.

SAM: Sure, Nancy.

NANCY: Well I better get moving, no use--

SAM: Wastin' yer time here, eh?

NANCY: If I come up with anything I'll let
            you know.

SAM: Thanks, an old man like me needs all
            the help I can get.

                    *(NANCY exits out office door.
                    SAM clears desk, gets up to put
                    on hat and coat)*

            Kenji was whistling in the dark, and
            Mackenzie's warning about the Tongs
            was so much warmed over B.S. As for
            the Wing kid, I'd seen her kind
            before. Another model minority
            expecting Powell Street to be a walk
            in the park, like she was doing us a
            favour by coming down to the dump.
            (pause as he pulls out note) That
            only left this note to tie in. I
            figured the hakujin guy at Rosie's
            was in on the Ides. If he had a hand
            in the disappearance of the Queen...
            then I was in business.

                    *(SAM exits out office door and
                    lights crossfade to Rosie's
                    Cafe. ROSIE is cleaning the
                    counter. CHUCK and SAM arrive.
                    CHUCK is carrying an umbrella)*

CHUCK: Hi Rosie.

ROSIE: Kombanwa. (Good evening.) *(goes to get menus)*

SAM: *(brushing off water)* What's hot tonight, Rosie?

ROSIE: Have you heard, Samu?

SAM: No, that's why I asked.

> *(CHUCK puts down umbrella and goes to sit at table. SAM hangs up his coat and pauses before deciding to keep hat on)*

ROSIE: *(giving menu to CHUCK)* Everybody is talking about Miss Lily Kudo. She's disappeared and no one can find her.

CHUCK: *(looking at menu)* You think the kid's a runaway?

ROSIE: Well, Watanabe-san says he heard Lily talking about going to Hollywood.

CHUCK: Doesn't sound likely, Rosie.

ROSIE: Sato-san says Lily ran away with her boyfriend-yo, because her daddy no like him.

SAM: *(walks over to table, takes a seat)* Only problem is John's at home, all broken up. I'll take the special.

CHUCK: *(closes menu)* Make that two. *(to SAM)* Who was the last to see her?

ROSIE: *(walking back to counter)* Goto-san says she saw Lily go to the dressing room.

SAM: That was about six thirty. Goto-san left a few minutes later.

ROSIE: And nobody see her again.

CHUCK: What about the room?

SAM: The forensic boys had combed the joint by the time I got there.

CHUCK: I got some friends down at the labs.

SAM: You better get on them.

ROSIE: *(returning to table to serve food)* You think maybe somebody kidnap Lily?

SAM: That's possible, plenty of henna hakujin (crazy white guys) running loose, eh.

CHUCK: Looks good, Rosie.

ROSIE: Thank you, Chuck-san. You should come here more often. I cook plenty for you too.

SAM: He's on a diet.

ROSIE: Honto?

SAM: Highballs and caviar at Chez Victor's.

ROSIE: Samu, you're pulling my leg again.

SAM: I've been meaning to do that for a long time. *(hits ROSIE on her behind)*

ROSIE: Oh Samu, kichigai neh! (Oh Sam, you are kinky!) *(walks back to counter)*

SAM: By the way, you remember that guy here this morning?

ROSIE: Hai, he come here sometime. He was at the Bazaar.

CHUCK: Got a suspect?

SAM: Just a hunch, about the Ides note.

CHUCK: Oh yeah?

SAM: He was sitting right there when I came in this morning.

CHUCK: How'd he stuff the note in your hat?

SAM: He paused at the rack before he walked out, plenty of time to plant it.

CHUCK: You know the guy, Rosie?

ROSIE: He call himself Gold something... speak very nice nihongo (Japanese).

SAM: Yeah, so I noticed.

CHUCK: Wouldn't be Goldfinger, would it?

SAM: Go ahead and chuckle Chuck, I'll bet on my hunch.

(NANCY enters)

NANCY: Well, we meet again.

SAM: You're on the job, rain or shine, eh kid?

(CHUCK stands up)

NANCY: *(taking off coat)* Don't let me interrupt you, I just dropped by for coffee.

CHUCK: *(to SAM)* You been holding out on me partner.

SAM: That's what you think.

CHUCK: Every man for himself eh. Hi, I'm Chuck Chan, Sam's legal advisor.

NANCY: Coffee please. I'm Nancy Wing, a reporter for the *Sun*.

CHUCK: Oh, I see.

NANCY: What?

CHUCK: Why Sam didn't introduce us.

NANCY: I'm sure he has his reasons. *(sits in CHUCK's chair)*

CHUCK: I call them grudges. He doesn't trust the press. *(gets a third chair)*

NANCY: So I notice.

CHUCK: Wing hmmm, you related to Wing Sum Chow by any chance?

NANCY: He's my great-uncle.

CHUCK: Now there's a hell of a pioneer. I
           used to run into him down at the King
           Hong Cafe.

NANCY: I don't know him very well.

CHUCK: I haven't seen you in Chinatown, have
           I?

NANCY: It's not my usual beat, I grew up in
           Richmond...and just because I'm
           Chinese--

SAM: Don't mean nothin', right kid?

NANCY: Well it doesn't mean I hang out on
           Pender Street.

SAM: Wouldn't want to attract the wrong
           kind of attention, eh?

NANCY: You know, you have a way of saying
           things that can get on someone's
           nerves.

CHUCK: Don't worry about Sam here, that's
           just his sense of humour.

NANCY: I don't hear anyone laughing.

CHUCK: That's because it's not very funny...
           Uh, you're new at the *Sun*?

NANCY: I started in January.

SAM: *(getting up)* Gochiso (Thanks) Rosie.

ROSIE: Domo Samu. (Oh, thank you, Sam.)

NANCY: Leaving already?

SAM:	I got business to take care of.
CHUCK:	You gonna talk to the other contestants?
SAM:	Yeah.
NANCY:	Might as well save your breath.
CHUCK:	They disappear too?
NANCY:	They're only talking to the police.
SAM:	They didn't welcome you with open arms, eh?
NANCY:	I suppose you know them personally.
SAM:	Better still, I know their parents... See you later, Rosie. *(exits)*
CHUCK:	I got a cousin in Richmond. You know a Harry Chan?
NANCY:	*(gets up)* There are a hundred Chans in Richmond.
CHUCK:	Yeah...you didn't touch your coffee.
NANCY:	You can have it...I gotta run.
CHUCK:	Say, do you like Japanese food?
ROSIE:	*(clearing table)* You want eat again?
NANCY:	Thanks...but no thanks. *(exits)*
CHUCK:	*(puts on coat)* Can't win 'em all, eh Rosie.

        *(CHUCK exits and ROSIE goes out
through the kitchen curtain as
lights crossfade to SAM's
office where he's typing at
desk)*

SAM: The other girls talked all right, but
they didn't have much to say. I
wasn't worried because there were
plenty of other witnesses to check
out. There was always the chance
that a lunatic had snatched the
Queen, but if the Ides note was a
threat to keep me off the case, then
the disappearance was part of a
bigger deal.

        (Knock on door. NANCY enters)

NANCY: Anybody home?

SAM: Look kid, don't you ever let up?

NANCY: I can't. This case is getting on my
nerves.

SAM: It's getting on mine too.

NANCY: I saw the light on and wanted to
check with you about the other
contestants.

SAM: We partners or something?

NANCY: Couldn't we cut the sarcasm a little?

SAM: Look kid, ain't it a bit late for you
to be out on the streets?

NANCY: I can take care of myself.

SAM: You put up a tough front, kid, but muggers take yah from behind. *(gets himself a drink)*

NANCY: I get the feeling your ideas about women are bit dated.

SAM: Maybe they are, I gave up on them a while ago. *(returns to desk)*

NANCY: So I've heard.

SAM: You been pumping Rosie, or Chuck?

NANCY: It doesn't take much to get them going on you.

SAM: Yeah, well I better set them straight about talking to strangers.

NANCY: They went on and on about the crimes you've solved and how you didn't charge much.

SAM: I don't need a press agent, kid.

NANCY: I could do an article on the way you broke up the teenage gang snatching purses from seniors around here.

SAM: Forget it, it was just a couple of dumb kids.

NANCY: Aren't you interested in getting any credit for your work?

SAM: Word of mouth goes far enough down here.

NANCY: Have it your way.

SAM: That's the way I like it.

NANCY: *(pause)* I bet this late night
              routine wasn't too popular with your
              wife.

SAM: My ex-wife... Now if the interview
              is over.

NANCY: You're always trying to get rid of
              me. I mean for two days you've acted
              like I had some social disease.
              (sits in client's chair)

SAM: I ain't used to having a woman waltz
              in here and shoot from the hip.

NANCY: What do you want, bound feet?

SAM: That's up to you kid, but you'd get
              a lot further by paying a bit of
              respect to your elders.

NANCY: You're not that old, Sam. I mean you
              don't look that old.

SAM: Thanks. *(finishes drink)* I'm well
              preserved.

NANCY: I get along with Chuck and I think
              Rosie even likes me.

SAM: Chuck's just a smooth talker and
              Rosie's the kind that takes in stray
              cats, so it's no use tryin' to use
              them to get to me.

NANCY: I'm not tryin' to get to you.

SAM: Then what have you been doing on my
              tail?

NANCY: I'm a reporter, and you're the only
          one who's got a handle on this case.
          At least this is the only place I can
          get my foot in the damn door!

SAM: It's tough getting inside when they
          know you want to get the story out
          there, eh? These people talk to me
          because they know I'll deal with it
          quietly.

NANCY: Do it the Japanese way?

SAM: *(walks to window)*   Think what you
          like kid.

NANCY: But I'm trying to help. Getting the
          facts to the public can help.
          Somebody might read the story and
          have something click.

SAM: The only click the papers want to
          hear is the quarter in the slot, and
          they've never been fussy about the
          facts.

NANCY: You're paranoid. The whole community
          is paranoid!

SAM: We've been screwed by your kind
          before.

NANCY: Is that my fault?

SAM: You're only a stringer, kid. The
          editors call the shots.

NANCY: *(gets up to leave)*   Thanks for
          nothing.

SAM: *(looking out window)* Turn out the light.

NANCY: Huh?

> *(She turns out light. Window shattering sound and SAM falls backwards as if hit by bullet. Sound of footsteps in hall)*

Sam!

> *(MACKENZIE and KADOTA rush into the office)*

MACKENZIE: Don't move!

NANCY: It's Sam, he's hit! *(kneels by him)*

KADOTA: Get the lights on!

MACKENZIE: Where's the switch?

NANCY: By the door, hurry, somebody call an ambulance!

SAM: No I'm all right! I'm only cut.

KADOTA: *(turns on light)* Mackenzie, check outside.

MACKENZIE: Aye, Captain. *(exits)*

KADOTA: You better get your nose fixed. *(goes to window)*

SAM: *(sits in chair, head back)* You shoulda told me yah had the joint staked out. I'd've sent out for coffee and sandwiches.

KADOTA: I told you we'd be around.

NANCY: Here let me help. *(goes to sink to get wet cloth)*

SAM: Thanks. *(takes cloth and wipes nose)*

KADOTA: Who did it, Sam?

SAM: That's confidential, Kenji.

KADOTA: You gotta play tough guy, nah.

SAM: I'll live longer that way... *(to NANCY)* Thanks... So what have you got on the Kudo case? *(gets up, walks to sink and puts Band Aid on nose)*

KADOTA: Nothing. A hundred witnesses and my own squad men at the scene, and the damn Queen disappears!

SAM: Funny, eh?

KADOTA: Maybe people are talking to you. You've been down here long enough.

SAM: You make it sound like doing time.

KADOTA: Are you going anywhere?

SAM: I never did have your ambition, Kenji. You must be bucking for another citation.

KADOTA: You're so clever, nah.

SAM: Just my way of staying sane.

KADOTA: Well I'm telling you, Sam, if you're withholding evidence I'll make you pay for it.

SAM: You're getting edgy.

KADOTA: Maybe I am, just watch out.

MACKENZIE: *(returning)* Not a blasted thing to report, Captain. I didna' see a shadow.

SAM: That's tough at night, eh Sarge.

MACKENZIE: Blimey, Captain, I'm gonna—

KADOTA: Call the lab boys, I want this place dusted for the bullet.

SAM: Maybe they could clean out my drawers too.

MACKENZIE: Why don't we run Sammy here downtown. He's holding out on us, ain't he? I can tell that.

KADOTA: You can't tell shit from gravy, Mackenzie. Now get on the phone.

MACKENZIE: Now that's a bit much, Captain. There's no call to play high and mighty with me.

KADOTA: Who's running this investigation anyway?

MACKENZIE: I was just speaking me mind!

SAM: *(sitting down at desk)* You two considered seeing a counsellor?

KADOTA: Mackenzie, do your job.

MACKENZIE: *(pause)* Aye, Captain, I'll do a job.
              (picks up phone)

SAM: Tough getting decent help these days,
              eh?

KADOTA: You keep quiet.

SAM: Sure.

MACKENZIE: Mackenzie here.

KADOTA: Man can't think with all that yapping
              going on.

SAM: So how's Superintendent Jameson?

KADOTA: What?

MACKENZIE: Could yuh send over the lads from the
              lab?

SAM: I heard he paid you a visit today.

KADOTA: So what?

MACKENZIE: Sniper fire.

SAM: Heard he wanted to see how you were
              handling the natives.

MACKENZIE: Right, over at Shikaze's office.

KADOTA: He gave me his solid support.

SAM: And forty-eight hours.

KADOTA: You got big ears.

MACKENZIE: What's that?

SAM: Let's say I got friends... What happens if you don't solve the case?

KADOTA: What do you mean?

MACKENZIE: Don't know, lad.

SAM: I heard you might get transferred to the Vice Squad. Who knows, we could be covering the same keyholes.

KADOTA: You're such a smart guy, nah.

MACKENZIE: Aye, you're right there.

SAM: Not me, Kenbo. I didn't finish cadet school, remember?

KADOTA: Yakamashi! (Shut up!)

MACKENZIE: *(hanging up phone)* Captain?

KADOTA: Now what, Mackenzie?

MACKENZIE: They're on the way.

NANCY: Same for me boys. *(heads for door)*

SAM: Thanks for the nose job.

NANCY: Anytime.

KADOTA: You better not print anything you just heard.

NANCY: I won't, if I don't make my deadline. *(exits)*

KADOTA: Let's go.

> (KADOTA and MACKENZIE exit.
> Lights come down to spot on
> SAM at desk)

SAM: The lab boys kept me up all night,
            turning the joint inside out. I
            showed them where the slug was buried,
            but they had to touch everything else
            too. Somebody was jumping the gun on
            the Ides, and that was fine by me,
            'cause nervous guys make mistakes,
            and that's how I nail them. I spent
            the next twenty-four hours questioning
            every possible witness at the Bazaar.
            It looked like a dead-end street till
            Rosie tipped me to a Mrs. Omoto.

> (Lights crossfade to Rosie's
> Cafe. SAM enters as ROSIE
> prepares to take food out)

            Hi Rosie.

ROSIE: Ah Samu, can you watch cafe for me?

SAM: Sure, I always wanted to be a waiter.

ROSIE: Haha...domo... Itekimasu. (I'm
            going.)

> (ROSIE exits. CHUCK enters)

CHUCK: Hey, I heard you had a close call the
            other night.

SAM: Yeah, seems like everybody is trying
            to take care of me.

CHUCK: You bring out the urge in people.

SAM: Must be huh.

CHUCK: *(goes to counter)* Where's Rosie?

SAM: Running breakfast to a few seniors down the street.

CHUCK: Any cracks in the mystery? *(goes behind counter to get coffee)*

SAM: I got a Mrs. Omoto who says she thinks she saw a hakujin man walk into the dressing room about six-thirty.

CHUCK: She thinks she saw?

SAM: The men's room is the next door down the hall. She can't recall which one he went in.

CHUCK: You know that won't stand up in court. *(returns to sit at table)*

SAM: She can hardly stand up... She's eighty-two with weak eyes and a bad memory.

CHUCK: Where'd you dig her up?

SAM: Through Rosie.

CHUCK: You ought'a put her on the payroll.

SAM: Yeah. *(pause)* You got the rundown on the other two cops at the Bazaar?

CHUCK: Yeah, Jeff Hori is a sansei from Steveston. He just married his high-school sweetheart and talks like a young Kadota.

SAM: Another token, huh.

CHUCK: The flip side is Rolf Pendersen. His nickname is "The Swinging Swede" 'cause he likes to play Tarzan with the women.

SAM: Mrs. Omoto said the guy was big so Pendersen could be our man.

(NANCY enters)

NANCY: Well, how goes the dynamic duo?

CHUCK: *(getting up to let her sit down)* That was some story in yesterday's paper.

NANCY: Thanks. *(sits down)* The public's got a right to know when the mayor's playing politics with ethnic issues.

SAM: From "ghettos" to "ethnic issues", eh kid? You're movin' fast.

NANCY: I'm doing my homework.

CHUCK: You've got the mayor and the superintendent dodging the media.

SAM: You may not have any friends soon.

NANCY: I'm not in this to make friends.

SAM: Pretty hard-nosed about it, aren't yah?

NANCY:	How's yours?
SAM:	It's still here.
NANCY:	That's nice to see. It'd be difficult snooping around without one, wouldn't it?
SAM:	Wouldn't know, I never tried it that way.

(ROSIE enters, carrying an empty tray)

CHUCK:	Hi, Rosie.
ROSIE:	Oh Nancy-chan, you looks so pretty, neh Chuck-san?
CHUCK:	Sure Rosie...
NANCY:	Coffee please.
SAM:	*(to CHUCK)* Did Pendersen mention going to the john?
CHUCK:	Yeah, he even said he bumped into Mackenzie on the way out.
NANCY:	What are you getting at?
SAM:	Nothin'.
CHUCK:	By the way, the lab boys found traces of Shiseido face powder in the closet, the same type Lily used.
NANCY:	You mean somebody might have put her there temporarily?

ROSIE: Who put Lily there? *(enters with coffee for NANCY)*

SAM: If we knew that we'd all be celebrating.

ROSIE: I hope we celebrate sugu (soon), neh. Everybody is crazy talking about Miss Lily Kudo... Oh Samu, did you talk to Omoto-san?

SAM: Oh yeah, thanks.

NANCY: Who's Omoto-san?

SAM: A ninety-year-old issei widow.

ROSIE: *(returning to kitchen)* Hachi ju ni. (Eighty-two.)

SAM: Eighty-two then.

NANCY: She know something, Rosie?

SAM: She sees things nobody else does.

NANCY: She a psychic?

SAM: Could be.

NANCY: Maybe I better check her out for myself, seeing as we're being so cryptic this morning.

SAM: Be my guest.

NANCY: You know where she lives, Rosie?

ROSIE: Hai, at the Lion Hotel, down the street. Be careful-yo, it's so kusai

(smelly) in there, and full of junk.
There's no room to sit down.

NANCY: Thanks, Rosie. Excuse me, boys, I
got a story to cover. *(exits)*

CHUCK: She doesn't wait for anybody, does
she?

SAM: You tryin' to make time with her?

CHUCK: You kidding? She hasn't got any to
spare.

SAM: It'll take her some time to figure
out Mrs. Omoto's story. The old lady
doesn't speak a word of English.

*(GOLDBERG enters and takes a
seat at the counter)*

ROSIE: Ohayo gozaimasu. Irasshaimas.
(Good morning and welcome.)

GOLDBERG: Ohayo gozaimasu. Ochazuke kudasai.
(Good morning, rice soup please.)

SAM: That's some fancy Japanese.

GOLDBERG: Sumimasen? (Excuse me?)

SAM: You speak English, buddy?

GOLDBERG: Oh yes, my name's Goldberg. I'm a
Japanese specialist.

SAM: Fascinating, ain't we.

GOLDBERG: Well...yes, Japanese is. It has a
certain simplicity and yet the most
subtle complexity.

SAM: So you're into things Japanese, eh?

GOLDBERG: I appreciate refinement.

SAM: How'd you like the Cherry Blossom
            Bazaar?

GOLDBERG: Oh charming, not an authentic
            Japanese ritual of course.

SAM: Chow mein and plastic lanterns eh.

GOLDBERG: Unfortunately, but I do like to speak
            to the old people.

SAM: *(getting up)* By the way, you ever
            heard of the Ides of March?

GOLDBERG: The what?

SAM: The Ides of March.

GOLDBERG: That's not Japanese.

SAM: You're right there, buddy. *(walks
            toward GOLDBERG)*

GOLDBERG: Well I believe it's some sort of
            ancient pagan ritual.

SAM: Like kidnapping queens?

GOLDBERG: I don't know what--

SAM: And planting threats?

GOLDBERG: This is absurd!

SAM: *(face to face)* You wouldn't know
            anything about this here note, would
            yah?

GOLDBERG: What's the meaning of this?

SAM: Just what I want to know.

GOLDBERG: But I don't even know what it says.

SAM: What yah gettin' nervous about?

GOLDBERG: I don't know!

SAM: Yah said that before.

CHUCK: Take it easy Sam.

GOLDBERG: *(getting up)* Uh, domo arigato
              (thank you), I've got to be going.
              (exits)

CHUCK: The guy doesn't even look like a
              kidnapper.

SAM: You tryin' to tell me something,
              Chuck?

CHUCK: I got a feeling that guy's okay.

SAM: Yeah, well I don't like the feeling
              I'm getting.

CHUCK: Maybe it's just a coincidence.

SAM: What is?

CHUCK: The Ides note and Lily's disappearance.

SAM: Could be, but that's not the way I
              see it.

CHUCK: Yeah, well it's your business, eh?
           (gets ready to go) Come to think of
           it I better take care of my own.

SAM: You in a hurry?

CHUCK: Got a date with a half-million bucks.

SAM: Don't let me hold you up.

CHUCK: I'll drop by tomorrow... 'Bye Rosie.

                    *(CHUCK exits. Lights lower to
                    black with only a spotlight on
                    SAM at table)*

SAM: *(to audience)* The pieces were
           beginning to fall into place. The
           Omoto-san tip pointed at Pendersen
           but I still figured Goldberg was the
           wild card in the deck. I needed to
           nail one of them soon, 'cause I didn't
           want to face the Ides without the
           kidnapper in my hands. So I figured
           it was time to take a walk downtown,
           into the heart of the jungle.

                    SAM exits out cafe door.

                    Blackout.

Act Two

The Dover Inn, an
English-style pub. There
is a noisy pub soundtrack.
SAM enters through door.

SAM: I dropped by the Dover Inn, where
Pendersen hung out. The joint was
jumpin', so I eased myself into the
crowd and waited for the Swingin'
Swede to show up.

(SAM takes seat at counter.
MACKENZIE enters through door
and walks to downstage left
without seeing SAM. He
addresses the audience)

MACKENZIE: Hello lads, ready for the meetin'
tonight? Good, the Super'll give yuh
a fine talk tonight, take me word for
that... *(looks at watch)* We better
hurry though eh, drink up, we got
plenty to do. *(exits out curtain)*

SAM: *(to audience)* Mackenzie was up to no
good, so I decided to tail him instead
of waiting for Pendersen.

*(SAM exits out curtain and lights
go to black with dramatic music.
Lights come up in alley way.
SAM appears looking in window
in stage left wall)*

I followed the footsteps into a back
alley. They were holding a meeting
in a warehouse across the way. I was
about to check out the action when I
realized I wasn't alone.

*(Sound of footsteps. SAM backs
away from spotlight into
shadows. NANCY appears at
extreme right curtain and
begins walking cautiously
across the stage. SAM grabs
her from behind)*

Don't breathe or I'll bust yer arm.

*(NANCY bites into his hand and
gives him an elbow in the ribs)*

Owww!... Ough.

*(NANCY turns to swing at SAM
who catches her arm and twists
it back)*

NANCY: Jesus, Sam, whose side are you on?

SAM: *(holding hand)* You want to get hurt,
            kid?

NANCY: I wasn't planning on it.

SAM: That's quite a set of molars you got
            there.

NANCY: You scared me.

SAM: Shhhh...

> *(SAM and NANCY look in window as Superintendent JAMESON and MACKENZIE enter from curtain and stop)*

JAMESON: Everything shipshape?

MACKENZIE: Aye sir, I got them good and roused.

JAMESON: How many lads?

MACKENZIE: Forty sir.

JAMESON: Good enough. Forty sturdy blokes could turn this city into a battlefield, right Sergeant?

MACKENZIE: Right sir.

JAMESON: Right then, here we go.

> *(JAMESON walks to centre stage, addressing the audience as if it were a warehouse crowd. He begins low key and builds to a frenzy)*

Thank you, lads. I think you know who I am and what I stand for. And I know you wouldn't be here if you didn't share the same ideals, and hope, and faith. I know the thought of losing this land to foreigners gets your blood boiling, as it does mine. I know you're all sturdy blokes, ready, aye ready, to bash a

few heads and send them packing
across the Pacific. It was bad
enough the Japs were allowed to
return, but now we're being overrun
by these Chinamen. They're takin'
our jobs, buying our homes, stealin'
the very food from our mouths. Why,
we don't even have a Chinaman's
chance to survive if we don't raise
our hands now to drive them out! Aye,
this country is sick with yellow
fever. They are a disease poisoning
our bloodstream. And we are the
saviours, the white blood cells, the
first line of defense and the last
hope of civilization! We are the
Sons of the Western Guard, and we
must drive them out! Drive them out!
Now!... Thank you!...thank you for
this convenant of faith. Now let us
kneel and give thanks to our Maker
for blessing this gathering and your
generous donations to the cause...
Thank you, Lord, for bringing our
flock together in these troubled
times, and bless all those who would
be the soldiers of your faith, amen.
*(aside to MACKENZIE who has stepped
into background)* Sergeant, pass the
trays around and take care of the
rest. I've another gathering to
attend.

MACKENZIE: Aye sir. *(whispered)* When shall we
move the girl?

JAMESON: Saturday.

MACKENZIE: Right sir.

(MACKENZIE AND JAMESON exit as
spot comes down)

NANCY: Do you know who that is?

SAM: He kicked me out of cadet school.

NANCY: He's a raving lunatic! What a scoop!

SAM: Keep yer shirt on, kid. This one
            ain't over yet. I'll tail the
            Superintendent and you keep track of
            Mackenzie.

NANCY: Wait a second.

SAM: (pause) Got any other suggestions?

NANCY: (shakes head) I'll meet you
            tomorrow.

SAM: Just don't get caught, or print
            anything I wouldn't eh.

NANCY: Then what do I do for a living?

SAM: Sneak down back alleys.

            (SAM walks to stage right till
            lights are black. Then he
            walks back to spotlight for
            monologue)

            (to audience) The Super slipped out
            the side door and took off in his
            limo. I tailed him all over town.
            He gave his little pep talks in a
            West Georgia office tower, an
            eastside factory, and a British
            Properties mansion.

(While SAM talks two figures search his office)

The Sons of the Western Guard were on the move, an army of blue and white collars led by the likes of the Superintendent and backed by bigwigs upstairs. The sons of bitches were everywhere and it was obvious that Mackenzie's remark meant they'd kidnapped the girl. I headed back to the office to check their file and think about their scheme.

(Spotlight goes to black. SAM steps to door, his hand groping on wall in dark for light switch)

Goddamn switch.

(SAM walks in the dark toward his desk. Two figures in ski masks jump SAM. One is MACKENZIE; the other can be anybody)

MACKENZIE: Take that yuh yellow bastard!

THUG: We'll give yuh more than a bleedin' nose this time!

(They beat SAM and throw him into his chair)

MACKENZIE: Where yah been, Sammy?

SAM: To see the Queen, boys.

(MACKENZIE hits SAM)

THUG: Got any more smart answers?

SAM: *(pause)* Got any more questions?

MACKENZIE: Right, where's yer Kudo file?

SAM: This the Hong Kong Tong connection?

MACKENZIE: *(hits SAM)* Yuh best pay attention to me questions, Sammy, otherwise yuh might get hurt.

SAM: Bit early for the Ides ain't it?

MACKENZIE: Yer blabbering again Sammy. *(hits SAM)* Now where's the Kudo file?

SAM: *(pause)* The desk...bottom drawer.

MACKENZIE: Glad to see yuh show some common sense, Sammy. *(goes to the desk and uses flashlight to check file)* Nothin' here... So yuh don't know a bloomin' thing yet eh...not a bit of evidence to show for all yer snoopin' around. Why I'm a bit disappointed, yuh know... I was hopin' we'd have a reason to put yuh away.

SAM: Tough luck eh.

MACKENZIE: *(hits SAM)* Yuh should wise up, Sammy, and take a trip to yer homeland.

                    (MACKENZIE and THUG beat SAM then exit out door. Lights fade to black then come up again on the office. It is the next morning. SAM gets up

slowly and walks to sink.
Knock on the door)

SAM: Come on in.

            (CHUCK enters)

            Glad you could make it.

CHUCK: Somebody really did a number on you
            eh.

SAM: Yeah, I feel like a bruised banana.
            (sits down)

CHUCK: Who was it?

SAM: *(getting himself a drink)* Mackenzie,
            and a friend on a midnight ride.

CHUCK: What the hell was he after?

SAM: My Kudo file... Wasn't much there
            so they tried a bit of muscle on me.

CHUCK: What's going on, Sam?

SAM: Plenty... We hit the jackpot last
            night. The Superintendent, Mackenzie,
            and probably Pendersen are members of
            the Sons of the Western Guard.

CHUCK: You saying the Sons kidnapped the
            Queen?

SAM: They were talking about moving the
            girl tomorrow.

CHUCK: That's gonna be tough to prove in
            court. You'll need the girl and
            plenty more.

SAM: That's where you come in partner.
Can you get a tail on Pendersen?

CHUCK: No problem.

SAM: I've heard Mackenzie and him are
taking a fishing trip this weekend.
It's a cover to move the girl, so
I'm gonna get Kadota to keep Mackenzie
in town. Meanwhile we hope Pendersen
leads you to the girl.

CHUCK: You better hope they don't get
suspicious.

SAM: I'm gonna need a few bugs in here,
too.

CHUCK: I can get them set up this afternoon.
What you got in mind?

SAM: Round two with Mackenzie tomorrow,
where we get in our licks before the
Ides. *(goes back to desk)*

CHUCK: You solve that one yet?

SAM: Not quite, but I figure we'll settle
that one tomorrow. How about your
million dollar divorce?

CHUCK: Oh fine, hubby wants to settle out of
court, and we're in the money.

SAM: How'd you swing that?

CHUCK: We caught him red-faced with a babe
in high heels and handcuffs.

SAM: He a cop?

CHUCK: No, a judge.

SAM: They got more weirdos up there than
            down here.

CHUCK: You may be right. *(walks to window)*
            Nancy come by?

SAM: I'm expecting her. You looking for
            her?

CHUCK: Not particularly... How are you two
            doing?

SAM: I was just gonna ask you that.

CHUCK: She's not interested in me.

SAM: I thought you were the big game
            hunter.

CHUCK: She's sweet on you, Sam.

SAM: I'm old enough to be her father.

CHUCK: That's what I said.

SAM: Huh?

CHUCK: You've been around a long time.

SAM: Yeah.

CHUCK: She's sharp though. Different kind
            of woman.

SAM: I only know one kind.

CHUCK: You've been alone too long. Times
            have changed, so have the women.

SAM: I hadn't noticed.

CHUCK: You're still playing the rock, eh?

SAM: I've been alone all my life, even
            when I was married. The kid doesn't
            know me from nobody. Maybe she has
            got some nerve.

CHUCK: You're finally showing some respect.

SAM: But she's still hustling me for the
            big scoop.

CHUCK: *(opens briefcase and takes out bottle
            of Canadian Club)* You're as hard
            bitten as they come. Maybe this will
            soften you up.

SAM: Thanks...for the bottle.

CHUCK: *(walking to door)* I'll get on the
            bugs and the tail...and you give my
            regards to Nancy. *(exits out office
            door)*

SAM: *(to audience as he sits at desk)*
            You know, I had a hunch the kid was
            after more than one scoop. But the
            trouble with women is that they start
            out looking up to yah, then they move
            in and end up overhauling yer joint.
            They tell yah smokin's bad for yer
            lungs and sleeping in bed is good for
            yer back. I'd seen it all before,
            and if that's what the kid was after,
            she was in for a surprise. *(picks up
            phone to make call)* Captain Kadota
            please... It's Sam Shikaze... He's
            on his way over eh. Fine...

(Knock on the door)

Come on in.

KADOTA: What happened to you?

SAM: I was entertaining some friends last night.

KADOTA: I bet you've been snooping around, eh? And somebody jumped you.

SAM: Yeah, a pair of kangaroos.

KADOTA: I told you to let us do the job.

SAM: You already did.

KADOTA: Did what?

SAM: Nothin'.

KADOTA: You never learn, do you?

SAM: Oh I'm learnin' plenty, Kenji.

KADOTA: What do you know?

SAM: Enough to get myself a citation.

KADOTA: Don't joke Sam.

SAM: Would I kid you?

KADOTA: I'll give you a break. We put our evidence together and I'll make sure you get some credit in this case.

SAM: That's generous of you, specially with me holding all the aces.

KADOTA: You're so cool, nah. They shake you
          up and you're still a wise guy. I
          come here to make a deal, and you
          laugh in my face.

SAM: Come on, Kenji, my time is short.
          (gets up to look in file cabinet)

KADOTA: Your time? Who do you think you are,
          some big shot?

SAM: You're burning a short fuse, Kenbo.

KADOTA: I'm a Captain, Sam. I got twenty
          years.

SAM: Don't tell me. *(sits down)*

KADOTA: *(gets up)* You got no idea how hard
          I worked.

SAM: Sure, I know it was a long haul.

KADOTA: You know! You know how much shit I
          had to take to make it. Smiling when
          they called me "Kamikaze Ken", never
          saying a word when they passed me over
          for promotions. Twenty years!...
          Seventeen citations!... I should be
          a chief inspector by now.

SAM: Get a hold of yerself Kenji...

KADOTA: The sons of bitches, that mayor and
          superintendent. They tell me maybe
          somebody else can handle this case.
          Like I was dragging my feet. They
          give me this look like I'm covering
          up for the kidnappers. Like I was
          guilty too!

SAM: That's the way they think.

KADOTA: I don't solve this one and I'm washed up!

SAM: I know.

KADOTA: You know?

SAM: It's written all over your face.

KADOTA: I've sweat blood to make it, Sam, and I'll drag your ass downtown if I have to.

SAM: Don't threaten me, Kenji.

KADOTA: I'll run you through the wringer.

SAM: Chuck'll have me out in no time.

KADOTA: Not this time!

SAM: *(stands up to face KADOTA)* Look, Kenji, all these goddamn years you been riding me, telling me I should play by the book, work my way up slowly, like you. All these years I've been shrugging off your bullshit. So now that your ass is on the line, where are all the rules and regulations? Didn't you read the fine print where it says twenty years of loyal service don't mean piss in the wind, if you're nihonjin? You think they wouldn't put us away again if the chips were down! Don't you know they wrote the book for suckers like you!

KADOTA: Yakamashi!

SAM: That's right, Kenji, turn it off.

KADOTA: And what have you got to show for
            your life? Everybody wondering how
            you live, divorced and working in
            this crummy joint. You should hear
            what your buddies really say about
            you. They call you an oddball...a
            loser.

SAM: They call me when they need me.

KADOTA: Sure, and later they say you're a
            weirdo, an embarrassment to us all.

SAM: Least they can't fire me.

KADOTA: You're not worth firing!

SAM: *(sits down)* So why bother with me?

KADOTA: We go back to the war, Sam. Doesn't
            that count for anything?

SAM: We never had it so good, eh?

KADOTA: What about my wife and family?
            What'll I tell my kid?

SAM: Tell him the truth.

KADOTA: But he's a Boy Scout!

SAM: Maybe it's time you grew up.

KADOTA: Jesus, Sam, we're nihonjin (Japanese)!

SAM: *(stands)* What the hell does that mean to you? You ain't got the time of day for us, wouldn't be seen down in the dump without a clothes peg on your nose. Couldn't do an old man a favour, 'til your fucking ass is in a sling...then we're "Nihonjin"!

KADOTA: They're putting the screws to me, Sam.

SAM: They always have been.

KADOTA: Don't talk crazy, Sam... I need your help. *(slumps into chair)* Give me a break.

SAM: *(walks to desk to pour a shot for KADOTA)* Another break, huh... Have a shot... *(puts bottle down on desk)*

KADOTA: Domo. *(downs drink in one gulp)*

SAM: Okay...but yah gotta play the game my way.

KADOTA: *(pause)* Sure.

SAM: *(pause)* Mackenzie's off 'til Monday, right?

KADOTA: So what?

SAM: *(pours KADOTA another drink)* Never mind. Can you get him on duty tomorrow?

KADOTA: He'll be swearing up and down at me.

SAM: Don't worry about that.

KADOTA: What is this?

SAM: I'm calling the shots, remember.
(sits down at desk)

KADOTA: But who's the suspect? Give me a name and I'll pick the guy up myself. *(stands up)*

SAM: It ain't that simple. *(pause)* Has Mackenzie ever talked about Shakespeare?

KADOTA: Shakespeare?

SAM: Yeah, the writer.

KADOTA: Which paper he write for?

SAM: He never mentioned the Ides of March huh?

KADOTA: He never talked about that.

SAM: Okay... I want both of you here tomorrow night.

KADOTA: I want the kidnapper, Sam.

SAM: You'll have him.

(KADOTA exits. SAM speaks while sitting at desk. Crossfade to spot)

Kenji would never understand what was going down. He was the kind that believed the camps were a blessing in disguise. When they made it tougher on him, he put his nose to the wheel and pushed harder. Twenty years and seventeen citations later, and they were still screwing him.

(Lights crossfade back to the
office. NANCY enters)

Well, glad to see you didn't get
caught.

NANCY: *(staring at his face)* Are you all
right?

SAM: I'll live... You find anything out
last night?

NANCY: That cop Pendersen showed up later.
Mackenzie led them through a few
songs and they broke up at eleven.
I tailed Mackenzie home, and that was
it.

SAM: Not quite... But it doesn't matter.

NANCY: What do you mean?

SAM: Nothin'.

NANCY: What did you pick up on the
Superintendent?

SAM: *(gets up)* He's a busy guy. He had
three more meetings to make.

NANCY: You got the names and addresses?

SAM: In my head. *(gets file from cabinet)*

NANCY: So give.

SAM: Not yet.

NANCY: Wait a second, I thought we were in
this together.

SAM: That's what you thought.

NANCY: Look Sam, I held off today's edition because I thought we had a deal. I was getting a lot of pressure to print something, but I didn't... because I trusted you.

SAM: *(faces NANCY)* Then yah gotta trust me a bit longer.

NANCY: I could still make the Saturday paper.

SAM: Yeah, and blow our chance to scoop the bunch of them.

NANCY: More like blow the case wide open.

SAM: Sure kid, we tell them we got an eighty-two-year-old widow who's half blind and can't speak English as our key witness. We tell them we saw the Super and Sarge at a social club meeting. Hell, we can claim we heard them talk about moving a girl.

NANCY: Well why not?

SAM: That's hot stuff for a gossip rag like the *Enquirer*, but you better get your lawyers ready for a libel suit. We're close, but not close enough to make the charges stick. We don't nail them good, and they cover their tracks better. You think these bruises are bad? Go ahead and break the story. *(sits down)* You may never type again.

NANCY: Don't try to scare me.

SAM: I'm trying to protect you.

NANCY: So what do we do, sit on our hands 'til the sun shines around here?

SAM: In forty-eight hours you can deliver the whole scoop in the Monday morning edition.

NANCY: What's the catch?

SAM: *(holds up hands)* No strings attached.

NANCY: I got the urge to frisk you.

SAM: Give me a break, kid, I got more important things to take care of.

NANCY: Okay, it's a deal...but that makes us partners, right?

SAM: Sure, you'll have the kidnappers by the Ides of March.

NANCY: Ides of March?

SAM: Yeah, you can call it my M.O.

NANCY: You're a strange one Sam.

(MACKENZIE enters)

MACKENZIE: Well now, ain't we as cosy as two peas in a pod.

SAM: Thought you had the day off, Sarge.

MACKENZIE: I do. Not like you, eh Sammy? Now when was the last time yuh took a holiday?

SAM: Thirty years ago. We all went to summer camp...in the winter.

MACKENZIE: Aye, well it's a sad thing yuh had to return, eh? Nobody was lookin' forward to seein' your kind around here again. *(sits down)*

SAM: Must have been a big letdown eh.

NANCY: Jesus, Sam, you gonna put up with that bullshit from this oversized toad!

MACKENZIE: Yuh got a regular firebird for a sugar here.

NANCY: Watch your mouth before I stuff it with a story that'll make you choke.

MACKENZIE: Ah, yuh got another story for us, eh?

SAM: *(gets up)* Yeah, about a good cop who gets set up on the chopping block.

MACKENZIE: Yer talkin' gibberish, Sammy.

SAM: Man serves twenty years on the force, and suddenly the force ain't with him anymore. The top dogs tell him to solve a certain case or pack his bags and move down to the Vice Squad.

MACKENZIE: My heart's bleedin' for yer man, but if he don't know his bloomin' place, then he's gotta learn, ain't he? He can't be civil to the lads he works with, then maybe he's gettin' what's comin' to him.

SAM: You mean his partners are setting him up?

MACKENZIE: Now I didna' say anything like that. Yer puttin' words in me mouth again, turnin' em all around 'til yuh gets what yuh wants, that's it, ain't it?

SAM: *(stalking MACKENZIE)* But you wouldn't blame the partners if they did, would yah?

MACKENZIE: They did nothin' I'm tellin' yuh. And I'm warnin' yuh for the last time Sammy, keep yer bleedin' nose out'a this here case.

SAM: *(sneezes)* Achoo!... Damn nose... Got a hanky?

MACKENZIE: Sure. *(hands SAM his hanky)* Better take care of yer health.

SAM: Beware the Ides of March, huh.

MACKENZIE: Yer talkin' pretty fancy for your kind.

SAM: Too fancy for your kind, eh?

MACKENZIE: I knows me own language better than any foreigner.

SAM: You talkin' about English? *(switches hanky with another in his pocket)*

MACKENZIE: Well now yuh been very clever so far, and all it's got yuh is a bunch of bruises and funny sayin's.

SAM: *(sitting down)* Some guys think I'm cute.

MACKENZIE: Aye, we all know yuh got enemies.

SAM: Least I can tell my friends from my enemies, now. And you Mackenzie...

> *(SAM extends his hand. When MACKENZIE reaches out SAM puts the different hanky in MACKENZIE's hand)*

...thanks for the hanky.

MACKENZIE: So take a tip from me, take some time off and let those marks heal up proper now. *(stands)*

SAM: I was hopin' they'd scar, give my mug some character.

MACKENZIE: Yuh never learn, eh Sammy? I go out'a me way on me day off to give yuh some sound advice, and I get no appreciation at all.

SAM: No use cryin' over spilt milk, Sarge.

MACKENZIE: Aye, I'll leave yuh with yer nursemaid here, and a warning. Why don't yuh save yerself a lot of trouble and take a long trip back to your homeland.

SAM: Beat the rush back eh.

MACKENZIE: Yuh ken me words eh... Then yuh best take me advice. *(exits)*

NANCY: Sorry I almost blew our hand, but the goddamn nerve! *(turns away)* I bet he's even using the kidnapping to get rid of the Captain, and that's only the beginning.

SAM: Things are coming together, eh kid?

NANCY: Look, I'm not a kid. Maybe I am new at the business, and I've made my share of mistakes, but I've figured some things out for myself.

SAM: Yeah, you've come a long way.

NANCY: *(pause)* I never thought I'd hear that from you...

SAM: You're doing all right.

NANCY: *(walking toward SAM)* I feel like I've touched a soft spot in the bedrock.

SAM: Why don't we just stick to the story, you know, keep it simple.

NANCY: I didn't mean to distract you... But you don't ever take time off? Just to relax and talk about things...or even watch TV?

SAM: Yeah, at home.

NANCY: But you're never there.

SAM: Okay Nancy, what's on your mind?

NANCY: *(walking away)* Jesus Sam, do you have to be so abrupt? Is everything so cut and dry for you?

SAM: *(pause)* My wife said I'd dried up,
          that living with me was like dying
          of thirst in the desert.

NANCY: She didn't pull any punches, did she.

SAM: I heard a lot worse.

NANCY: But it doesn't have to be that way.

SAM: No, it didn't.

NANCY: I mean you care about people, like
          Rosie and Chuck.

SAM: That's different.

NANCY: It's only another way of caring.
          Maybe it wasn't your fault. Maybe
          it was the relationship, or your wife.

SAM: She had problems all right, but I was
          the biggest one. She wanted to
          entertain friends, and take long
          vacations, have a big house in
          Shaughnessey with me playing the
          breadwinner. She had plans to turn
          me into a somebody.

NANCY: I've talked to plenty of people around
          here, and they all look up to you.
          Not those stuff-shirt nisei hiding
          out in the suburbs, but the people
          who live around here. You can't
          measure that in dollars and cents.
          Your wife couldn't understand what
          you were doing!

SAM: So what are you getting worked up
          about?

NANCY: I don't know.

SAM: What'd I do now?

NANCY: Nothing... That's the problem. Don't
           you feel anything through that thick
           skin of yours?

SAM: Yeah, I've been here before... I got
           a knack for upsetting women.

NANCY: Jesus Christ!

SAM: Look, Nancy, you're an attractive
           young woman.

NANCY: You sound like somebody's uncle...
           Sam...I care about you.

SAM: *(pause)* Yeah, *(pause)* I could see
           you comin' a mile away. You were so
           busy winding yourself up for the big
           romance that you forgot one thing:
           you don't know me from nobody. To
           you I'm somebody who looks good in a
           back alley when you're scared. You
           want a hero but you're just setting
           yourself up for the fall.

NANCY: That's my business, Sam. You think
           you're the first guy in my life?
           I've been around and I can take care
           of myself. Maybe I am looking for a
           hero, somebody with character... Who
           the hell isn't!

SAM: That makes great copy kid, but what
           else have I got? A one room walkup
           with no closet space? You want to
           listen to music on a beat-up old

radio? Make out on a lumpy mattress?
You think we got a chance of lastin'
five minutes beyond this case?

NANCY: It doesn't matter. I've got my own
           career and space. We don't have to
           live together.

SAM: You're the liberated type eh.

NANCY: Does it have to be love and marriage,
           or love 'em and leave 'em? Isn't
           there room in your life for a mature
           relationship between consenting adults?

SAM: That was a mouthful kid, and maybe
           that's your style, but I got my own
           way of doin' things.

NANCY: I can see that, but isn't there any
           room for the two of us to share?

SAM: Give me a breather kid, we gotta
           think about this first.

NANCY: At least you're talking we now.

SAM: Why me? You could have your pick of
           the hot shots downtown. Chuck could
           go for you, and he's more your age.

NANCY: I'm looking for someone older,
           someone who's been around, knows the
           score the way you do.

SAM: What do you want, a father?

NANCY: That's not what I had in mind.

SAM: I'm getting nervous, kid.

NANCY: I mean it. You don't want or need
          the things most guys do to feel good
          about themselves. You don't need a
          flashy car or a new office or fancy
          women to stroke your ego. You don't
          need things to protect you from the
          world out there. You're different,
          you're weird... You're down here on
          Powell Street because you want to be,
          you're not hiding out, you're just
          living here, like somebody who doesn't
          care if the world passes him by,
          because the world isn't going
          anywhere!

SAM: Who would've believed this eh, an old
          guy like me makin' time with someone
          like you.

NANCY: Sam, I'm gonna scream if you call
          yourself old again. You're in the
          prime of your life.

SAM: Maybe I'd rather not think about that.

NANCY: Why not?

SAM: (pause) 'Cause you start lookin'
          over your shoulder at how easy it
          used to be. You turn forty and
          you're still alone, and suddenly the
          old hot plate doesn't heat up enough
          to boil water. You get up and stare
          at the walls around you and wonder
          what's the use. You want to know why
          I spend all my time here? 'Cause
          this is where I live, this is what I
          call home... This is all I got!

NANCY: Sam...

SAM: You want to know where these bruises came from? A couple of goons jumped me, right here in my own goddamned office! Twenty years ago I would have wiped the floor with their asses ...and last night they kicked mine. *(pause)* The prime of life? Who're you kidding? It's the edge, and when you look out there it's dark, and fear turns your insides.

NANCY: But you don't change. You just go on.

SAM: You're too young to understand.

NANCY: You're not afraid of growing old alone. You're afraid of me, afraid of having to wake up and feel again. You want to go out like some dirty old butt! Look at you, look at this place! You've grown comfortable here, surrounded by "The Community", by Mrs. Tanaka and her crazy son, by old man Shimizu and his lost wallets, by Mr. Kudo and his missing daughter. You look at me and all you see is trouble, somebody who doesn't fit into your little world!

SAM: What the hell do you want?

NANCY: You! The guy that calls his own shots.

SAM: *(pause)* I don't know, it's been a long time.

> *(SAM walks to spotlight. NANCY walks up behind him)*

NANCY: Not that long. *(pause)* You know you're pretty good looking when you get going.

>   *(Office lights come down as spotlight comes up on them. SAM reaches out and pulls NANCY to him)*

SAM: You don't let up...do you?

>   *(They kiss as music begins)*

NANCY: I like to think I get my man.

SAM: You and the Mounted Police, eh?

NANCY: They got nothing on me.

SAM: Well, you just about got this one.

NANCY: That's not good enough.

SAM: All right, I give up...

>   *(They kiss. Music continues as they exit out office door. Lights go to black. A light comes up in the office and SAM enters)*

SAM: *(to audience)* The kid was as good as her word. We started out in the office and ended up at her joint. It wasn't so bad after all. The only problem was, we blew the rest of the afternoon and night. I figured the morning after was going to be rough, but the kid made a decent bowl of juk to settle my insides. *(pause)* I dropped by the labs that afternoon to have them run a few tests on Mackenzie's hanky. If my hunch was right, the showdown wasn't gonna wait for the Ides.

(NANCY enters)

NANCY: I still think we should go after the Superintendent.

SAM: But Sarge is the weak link.

NANCY: And who's taking care of the Queen?

SAM: Chuck is.

NANCY: What's that? *(looking at what SAM's working at)*

SAM: A bug, so just remember your lines and we'll nail his ass.

(Knock on the door. MACKENZIE and KADOTA enter)

KADOTA: Evening, Sam.

SAM: Evening, boys.

MACKENZIE: What's going on? I had a holiday comin' to me. I ought'a be out fishin' right now.

SAM: Hardworking Japanese don't believe in holidays. Right, Kenji?

MACKENZIE: What's yer game, Sammy?

SAM: I've decided to come clean.

KADOTA: Right, Sam.

MACKENZIE: Well ain't that a change? Tough guy
               turns law-abidin' citizen. Yer
               sweetheart put yuh up to this?

SAM: Not this time, Sarge.

NANCY: You see, Mackenzie, we think
               Pendersen did it.

KADOTA: Pendersen?

MACKENZIE: Yer off the mark there. He's an
               honest sort of bloke if ever there
               was one. Why he's my drinkin' mate,
               and we was supposed to go fishin'
               together.

KADOTA: You know what you're sayin', Sam?

MACKENZIE: And how could he 'ave done it? We
               was there together with that Jeff
               Hori. Look to yer own kind, why
               don't cha! Now there's a sneakin'
               sort. Always smilin' and real quiet
               like. Walks like a cat, can't hardly
               hear him come up behind yuh. Can't
               drink without turnin' all red. Now
               he'd have a reason to snatch the
               Queen.

NANCY: He had relatives at the Bazaar who'll
               swear they were talking to him all
               the time.

MACKENZIE: How can yuh take their word for that?
               They're the same kin, ain't they?

SAM: Witnesses say Pendersen went to the
               john about six-thirty.

MACKENZIE: So now it's a crime to go to the convenience.

NANCY: He used the washroom as a cover. On his way out, after he ran into you, he ducked into the dressing room.

MACKENZIE: But the girl didn't scream.

SAM: Why would she, he was a cop.

MACKENZIE: Then I suppose he charmed her into a Houdini act?

SAM: That's where this hanky comes in. *(pulls out hanky)*

MACKENZIE: Huh?

SAM: We figure it belongs to Pendersen. The lab tests show traces of ether and face powder. The ether to knock the girl out, and the face powder matches the type she used. *(puts hanky back in pocket)*

KADOTA: Honto!

MACKENZIE: Very clever, Sammy. I always said yuh was the one to watch. But what next?

SAM: Everybody, including Pendersen, leave. The Bazaar is over, the father thinks the boyfriend took her home. All quiet in the Church. Then Pendersen gets off duty an hour later and returns to pick up the girl.

MACKENZIE: That's as sweet as a cup of tea.
Only Pendersen ain't the type to
kidnap women.

SAM: Right, they were usually after him.

MACKENZIE: Aye, he had a knack with them.

NANCY: We dug up another angle. He's a
member of the Sons of the Western
Guard. You're familiar with them,
aren't you?

MACKENZIE: I knows something about them.

SAM: Yeah, I suppose you do, seein' as how
you organize their meetings.

MACKENZIE: This is free country, ain't it?
Man's got a right to join a social
club.

NANCY: One that proclaims the supremacy of
the white race? That proposes Canada
should purge itself of alien races,
like Asians, and Jews, and Native
Canadians?

MACKENZIE: I got a right to me own opinions, and
what's that got to do with the
kidnapping?

KADOTA: Yeah, Sam.

SAM: We found out the Superintendent is
also an organizer for the Sons, the
kind that goes around and gives pep
talks to the faithful.

KADOTA: Now you're going too far, Sam.

MACKENZIE: Oh yer very thorough now, ain't yuh Sammy?

SAM: Pendersen and the Super hatched the plan to get rid of Kenji here.

KADOTA: Naniyo?

MACKENZIE: Yer talkin' gibberish, man. Who's gonna believe this wild goose chase about hankies and social clubs and plans to get rid of the Captain here?

KADOTA: *(to himself)* Mackenzie?

SAM: Speakin' of hankies, this one's yours. *(unfolds it to reveal initials)* Got your initials on it.

MACKENZIE: *(checking his own pocket to find the wrong one)* This one ain't mine. Why yuh sneakin' yellow bastard!

KADOTA: Mackenzie! My own partner.

MACKENZIE: *(draws gun)* Aye, I was yer partner, and a bit o' hell it was. Takin' orders from your kind. That weren't right at all. So we decided to fix yuh up good.

SAM: You and the Super and Pendersen.

MACKENZIE: Aye, we're the Sons, and proud of it ... We've been lettin' yer kind push us around long enough. Now we're gonna start pushin' back.

SAM: You kidnap the Queen, squeeze Kenji out of position, and later pin the rap on the Tongs.

MACKENZIE: And that's just the beginning. Like the Super says, we're gonna send yuh packin' across the Pacific.

NANCY: What happens to the girl?

MACKENZIE: Oh she's in good hands. We was gonna take her fishin'.

NANCY: You bastards!

> (NANCY and KADOTA step toward MACKENZIE)

MACKENZIE: Get back!

> (They step back)

SAM: Things are getting complicated though, eh Sarge?

MACKENZIE: I was just thinkin' about that, and I thinks maybe we can fix up a bit of an accident in this here fire trap.

KADOTA: No, Mackenzie.

> (KADOTA rushes MACKENZIE. MACKENZIE fires and hits KADOTA but KADOTA knocks him off balance. SAM jumps MACKENZIE. Then NANCY rushes to help KADOTA while SAM and MACKENZIE struggle. SAM gains control of the gun)

SAM: Back up, Sarge.

MACKENZIE: He was crazy!

SAM: You all right?

MACKENZIE: He jumped me, it was self-defense!

SAM: Don't worry, Kenbo, we'll get you to
                a hospital.

NANCY: I'll call an ambulance.

                (JAMESON enters holding a gun)

MACKENZIE   I wouldna' touch the tellyphone if I
                was you.

NANCY: What?

JAMESON: *(at door holding gun)* Maybe you
                better call the morgue instead.

SAM: *(putting up hands)* Shit.

MACKENZIE: *(taking gun from SAM)* Excellent
                timing sir, this is a bit of luck.

JAMESON: Luck my arsehole. Now get on the
                phone and ring up the mayor. *(taking
                gun from KADOTA)* Tell him we've had
                a bit of bad luck here, losing one of
                our best men.

MACKENZIE: Righto sir.   *(picks up phone)*

SAM: He always was a favourite of yours,
                eh?

JAMESON: And you're still the troublemaker.

SAM: What yah gonna call this one, a
                double murder-suicide?

84

MACKENZIE: Sergeant Mackenzie here, may I have a word with the mayor?

JAMESON: How does the Ides of March Massacre sound?

SAM: Like your kind of dirt.

JAMESON: You should have heeded the warning.

SAM: I got the message.

JAMESON: But you had to stick your nose in anyways eh.

SAM: Just for the record...who delivered the note?

JAMESON: You're dying to know, aren't you?... Well you should be more careful about getting your hat cleaned.

SAM: I will.

JAMESON: Too late, Shikaze, this is the final act with you playing the aging Romeo in a story about two middle-aged rivals squabbling over this pretty young thing. Such an exotic ending eh.

MACKENZIE: Uh, Mr. Mayor, sorry to disturb you sir.

NANCY: That could be difficult to explain with Sarge's gun as exhibit A.

MACKENZIE: Well we've had a bit of an accident.

SAM: Better let Sarge in on the plans before he blows his lines.

JAMESON: Just tell him to get down here!

MACKENZIE: At Shikaze's office sir, uhuh.

SAM: You're wastin' yer time, Sarge, he's
              not coming.

JAMESON: You're bluffing, Shikaze.

MACKENZIE: But sir, we need yuh here.

JAMESON: Tell him it's a multiple murder.

SAM: Tell him we've solved the kidnappings
              while you're at it.

MACKENZIE: No sir, yuh don't understand... I
              got nothin' to do with it!

JAMESON: What's he saying, Mackenzie?

MACKENZIE: Could yuh hold the line for a bit?

SAM: You boys want to hand over your
              pieces.

JAMESON: One more word out of you and it'll be
              your last.

MACKENZIE: Jesus...it's all over sir!

JAMESON: What are you blubbering about!

MACKENZIE: He says they got us surrounded...
              What'll we do!

SAM: Stiff upper lip, Sarge.

JAMESON: Get over to the window, we've still
              got hostages.

(CHUCK appears at door with gun)

CHUCK: Get 'em up boys.

JAMESON: *(turning)* Chan!

SAM: *(taking JAMESON's gun)* Relax, Jameson.

JAMESON: What's this about?

SAM: Shakespeare, buddy.

JAMESON: But I was about to get Mackenzie to
             lead me to the others.

MACKENZIE: What?

SAM: Nice try, but you aren't calling the
             shots anymore.

JAMESON: This is ridiculous. I'm the
             Superintendent of Police!

MACKENZIE: Aye, and the clan leader.

JAMESON: This man is obviously a lunatic!

SAM: What does that make you?

JAMESON: Listen to me...I can prove I've
             infiltrated the organization known
             as the Sons of the Western Guard.

MACKENZIE: Infiltrated? Why he's the bloody
             preacher, selling us all on his fire
             and brimstone ideas... He's the real
             looney bird!

SAM: Keep talkin' boys, I'm all ears.

JAMESON: We're closing in on the highest level of command.

MACKENZIE: Why the dirty ferret!

JAMESON: I can't name names right now.

CHUCK: That's pretty convenient, eh?

JAMESON: We can't trust anyone... Their agents are everywhere...even among your own people.

NANCY: *(to SAM)* This could be the tip of the iceberg.

SAM: That's what I don't like.

MACKENZIE: He's a sly one, Sammy.

JAMESON: Believe me, this blundering simpleton is only the willing tool of the powers that be.

MACKENZIE: Why yuh sneakin' weasel! *(lunges at JAMESON)*

SAM: *(grabs MACKENZIE)* Get back! Another move and I'll bust yer ass, 'cause I owe you, Sarge.

JAMESON: Take my word for it, gentlemen, his kind are dangerous. So we must move quickly. Pendersen still has the girl.

CHUCK: You mean he had the girl.

JAMESON: What?... Well, jolly good work, but you've wiped out six months of careful investigation.

SAM: We didn't mean to get in the way.

JAMESON: You've caught their thugs, and saved
                the girl, but you've let the bigger
                fish out of the net.

CHUCK: We've got you.

NANCY: Who are you working for?

JAMESON: Too much is at stake to expose the
                operation. Blowing my cover is not
                the only problem, there are others in
                more sensitive positions.

CHUCK: *(picking up phone)* Why don't we call
                up the Attorney General and find out
                who's giving the orders.

JAMESON: Wait!... I didn't want to say this,
                but the Attorney General is--

SAM: The honorary past president, right?

JAMESON: You must take this seriously, we are
                sitting on a bomb that will rock the
                government.

NANCY: This is one hell of a story.

SAM: Yeah, if we can get it straight.

MACKENZIE: Yuh can't even trust yer own kind
                anymore.

JAMESON: In twenty minutes I have a meeting
                with the Sons' national director.
                If you want to get the kingpins
                behind the organization, you'll let
                me continue my work.

CHUCK: Your move, Sam.

NANCY: You think the Attorney General's in
            the Sons?

SAM: Could be... *(takes gun out of desk)*
            Okay, Jameson, we'll give you some
            rope to play with... *(gives him gun)*
            Here, yah might need this.

JAMESON: What about mine?

SAM: I'm gonna run a check on it.

JAMESON: Smart move. *(smiles and raises gun)*
            But you can forget that.

NANCY: Oh no.

MACKENZIE: Christ Almighty, what's goin' on!

JAMESON: I saved our cause you idiot, now get
            their guns.

SAM: *(raises his gun)* Don't bother, Sarge.

JAMESON: *(pulls trigger of gun)*   Huh?

CHUCK: Looks like the rat went for the
            cheese.

MACKENZIE: Blimey, Sammy, yuh got us again!

SAM: *(taking gun)*   Sorry, Jameson, they
            only work when they're loaded.

JAMESON: You slithering bastard.

SAM: I ain't the one that's squirming,
            buddy.

CHUCK: That wraps it up, eh?

SAM: Almost.

NANCY: We'd better get the Captain to the
          hospital.

SAM: Oh yeah, got to take care of our own,
          right Super?

          *(Lights go to black with siren
          sounding in background. SAM
          stands in spotlight)*

SAM: Monday, March 30th, 1973. The Ides
          had come and gone. Miss Cherry
          Blossom was back in the mainstream.
          The Super, Mackenzie, and Pendersen
          were all plea bargaining in a case that
          was rocking the government. Chief
          Inspector Kadota was breaking in his
          new badge, and Chuck was downtown,
          making hay while the sun shines. As
          for the kid, she won some award for
          her scoop on the Sons, and got a fat
          offer from the Toronto *Globe and Mail*.
          That meant moving east. *(pause)* And
          she did, saying she'd give it a year.
          (pause) Chuck was right. She was a
          different kind of woman. *(pause)*
          And me? I dropped by Rosie's for some
          ochazuke and the latest news on Powell
          Street.

          *SAM walks out of spot into
          darkness. Spot comes down.*

          The End

Additional copies of YELLOW FEVER can be obtained for $4.95 each prepaid from PLAYWRIGHTS UNION OF CANADA. For other play titles, consult our free catalogue.

PLAYWRIGHTS UNION OF CANADA
8 York Street, 6th Floor
Toronto, Ontario
Canada M5J 1R2
Phone (416) 947-0201